I0607379

The Healing Kitchen

Ginger

Chives

Basil

ORGANIC HERB-GARDEN PANTRY,
SMART-FOOD RECIPES, AND
ALL-NATURAL REMEDIES BY

Patricia
Stapley

PHOTOGRAPHS BY LAURIE RUBIN

The Healing Kitchen

AN INDOOR HERB-GARDEN PHARMACY FOR COOKS

Sage

MACMILLAN • USA

Please note: This book contains at-home remedies, using herbs, essential oils, and an assortment of other ingredients that might cause allergic reactions to some individuals. Reasonable care in their preparation and use is advised. These at-home remedies are not for use by children or pets. Further, the at-home remedies are in no way to be considered as a substitute for consultation with a medical doctor.

MACMILLAN
A Simon & Schuster Macmillan Company
1633 Broadway
New York, NY 10019-6785

Copyright © 1996 by Fly Productions
Photographs © 1996 by Laurie Rubin

LIBRARY OF CONGRESS CATALOGING-IN-PUBLICATION DATA
Stapley, Patricia.
     The healing kitchen : an indoor herb-garden pharmacy for cooks / Patricia Stapley ; photographs by Laurie Rubin.
        p. cm.
    ISBN 0-02-860394-X
    1. Cookery (Herbs) 2. Herbs 3. Herb gardening. I. Title.
    [DNLM : 1. Herbs — Therapeutic use.]
TX819.H4S73 1996
641.6'57 — dc20
                          95-47405
                            CIP

Manufactured in the United States of America

10   9   8   7   6   5   4   3   2   1

F Y
PRODUCTIONS

For my Mother and Father, with love.

PHOTOGRAPHER'S ACKNOWLEDGMENTS & DEDICATION:

To my husband, Bruce, and my son, Cole, for all their late night studio visits. My gratitude to the extraordinary people with whom I work — Dave Mink, Jill Garrison, Tamara Staples, and Randi Fiat — you have my profound thanks. To Bonnie Rabert, who braved last summer's heat to grow the outstanding herbs that appear in my photographs. To Esther Mitgang, who gave me the opportunity to share my photographs in this, my second, book. To my folks — Ron and Deborah Rubin, for running, fixing, doing, fixing, juggling, waiting, and fixing — my gratitude and love.

Grown at home.

Nurtured to harvest.

From window sill to place setting:

Living food for

Living well.

Contents

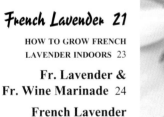

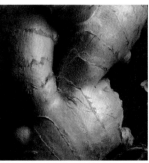

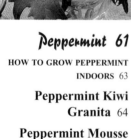

Introduction

Welcome to my healing kitchen. In the next few pages, I'd like to share some general information on the botanical, culinary, and therapeutic benefits of homegrown herbs to help you get started making your own indoor herb garden as healthy and useful as it is beautiful. The sixteen herbs showcased in *The Healing Kitchen* — sweet basil,

curly chervil, garlic chives, dill, French lavender, ginger, Italian parsley, lemon balm, lemon verbena, sweet marjoram, mizuna, peppermint, nasturtium, rosemary, sage, and thyme — are all cooperative houseplants, inherently aromatic, flush with flavor, and effective healers. Each herb is highlighted in a three-part, stand-alone chapter of its own, providing step-by-step indoor growing instructions (from ordering hardy seeds through harvesting an abundant, healthy crop); a quick, simply cooked recipe, featuring the herb's distinct aroma and delicious flavor as its centerpiece; and an easy-to-prepare, practical home remedy for relief of a common ailment or a self-care treatment for enhancing natural beauty.

Begin by establishing a well-run indoor planting station to nurture your herbs to thriving maturity. Dedicate a cool, dry cupboard, a shelf, a drawer, and a flat work surface (a kitchen table is just fine) to store the equipment and supplies you need on hand. Gather and organize the following: an indoor horticulture encyclopedia, several six-by-six-inch terra-cotta pots with matching saucers (the recommended size for nearly all the herbs you're growing), a variety of decorative, ceramic cachepots with drainage holes — an absolute must, a supply of small stones and broken clay pots in a sturdy, clean container, a large bag of all-purpose potting soil, a bag of sharp sand, a bottle of liquid plant food, a nonmetal watering can, a pair of sharp scissors, a small garden trowel, a collection of glass jars with screw-tops, and a roll of plastic wrap. (The growing instructions for each herb provides its planting procedures and environmental requirements in detail.)

Herbs, like most plants grown indoors, are sitting targets for airborne diseases and pests. At the first sign of illness, isolate the sick plant to prevent infecting the others and remove any damaged leaves. Consult your favorite indoor-horticulture book to identify and treat your plant's condition. If, after a week, your plant is not responding, call the seed company or nursery where you purchased the plant to seek professional advice.

No matter how abundant your indoor harvests are, your pantry planting is no doubt small, limiting your yield of useable leaves and flowers. Harvesting requires care. Never strip-harvest your herb plants. (Only chives like to be harvested crewcut-style.) I recommend pinch-harvesting to keep your plants bushy and productive. Some herbs want their growing tips plucked regularly to promote leaf growth and delay bolting. Others perish if their topmost tips are removed. Not to worry, I outline the specific harvesting method for each plant. While you wait for your herbs to mature to harvest (or, if you run out of homegrown bouquet garni), it's perfectly permissible to buy fresh herbs at the green grocer to use in the preparation of the recipes and remedies. (Of course, you're soon spoiled for the cream of the crop!)

The flavorful diversity of homegrown herbs color the simplest foods, turning ordinary dishes into extraordinary ones. The recipes in *The Healing Kitchen* spotlight the bright and lively taste of herbs at their fresh best.

To incorporate a living-herb pantry into the average kitchen doesn't take a lot of special cooking equipment (you probably have most of the following): multi-purpose glass jars with screw-tops, an assortment of tightly covered containers for refrigerator storage, a blender or food processor, and a sharp knife. If the preparation of a recipe (or a remedy) requires a unique item, that I think you may not have on hand, I bring it to your attention by including it on the list of ingredients.

Healing herb plants — our earliest medicines and cosmetics — are thankfully (and finally) being rediscovered and reappreciated. Pharmaceutical companies are responding to the public's demand for chemical-free, all-natural products. The trendiest beauty treatments now boast all-botanical ingredients. (Read the labels. Many of these products 'boast', but their labels reveal only trace amounts of the active herbal substances.) You can be sure of what you're using, if you make it yourself. All of us, even if we weren't aware at the time, have been exposed to natural remedies — a mustard plaster applied for a chest cold, a cup of herb tea to soothe an upset stomach, or a vaporizer, filling a sickroom with healing herbal steam.

The remedies in *The Healing Kitchen* are gently effective. With the exception of the Thyme Cough Drops, the Sweet Basil Balm, and the Italian Parsley Cleansing Tonic, all of the herbal treatments require the preparation of an infusion or a tincture. For convenience, these techniques are repeated, step-by-step, in the directions for each herbal remedy. The formulas for all of the remedies are mixed on the mild side to accommodate a wide range of people with diverse personal habits, lifestyles, and health histories.

A word of advice before you self-medicate. It's up to you to apply common sense and proceed with caution. Herbs are healing medicine. Perform skin tests, especially if you're sensitive, and consult a physician before trying to cure any lingering condition.

Now that the caveats are out of the way — organize your pantry pharmacy. Just like indoor-gardening and cooking, the right equipment at your finger tips makes preparation quicker and easier. Dedicate a cupboard and a drawer to store the supplies for your kitchen-remedy station: cheese cloth, sterile cotton gauze, surgical tape, an eye cup, a gallon jug of distilled water, amber glass and clear glass bottles with screw-tops and spray tops in an assortment of sizes, several glass jars with screw-tops, an eight-ounce bottle of almond oil, a small, nonmetal perfume funnel, a couple of glass droppers, a fine-gauge sieve, a nonmetal teapot, a ball of cotton kitchen string, a pair of sharp scissors, and a heavy-bottomed, nonmetal pot with a tightly fitting lid that's dedicated to preparing your remedial infusions.

Keeping my healing kitchen productive and efficient is a source of great personal joy. As you explore this world of natural goodness, I wish you wellness, savory flavor, and fruitful harvests.

Sweet Basil

Sweet basil's scent is so alluring, it makes perfect sense to include fragrant sprigs in a vase of cut flowers. The gem-colored leaves of this delightful member of the mint family range from emerald to amethyst, the aromatic nosegay of flavors from cinnamon to anisette to lemon. In the raw, coarsely chopped, the stand-up taste puts the zing in Thai-Style Relish.

Sweet basil's therapeutic properties are largely unsung. A Sweet Basil Balm of fresh leaves applied to cuts, scratches, and scrapes soothes, disinfects, and speeds healing. My choice, sweet or common basil, is at home indoors. A culinary classic, the sweet, clove-like flavor withstands cooking. Frequent pinch-harvesting keeps your plant productive for months.

daughter.

just the same

the engagement ring

bradley, music by others

no Body.

who sank with the Maine

trusting Lead in th

43.
44.
45.
46.
47.
48.

kama" Coon

who sank with the Maine

the Mistletoe Bough

mid, the green

my mamma there   52

53 Kiss, and let's m

of Daisies   54.

sweet   55 I dont want

56.

57.   the village

58

59.

Recruits Soliloquy   60

than Gold.   61

your Gold.   62

63.

Sweet, or common, basil (*Ocimum basilicum*) is a happy indoor herb. Of the twenty or more species, sweet basil is this chef's choice. I recommend growing the

Botany, briefly

Genovese variety for its pungent aroma and flavor. The seeds are available year-round from seed catalogs.

Your healthy sweet basil plants produce a long tap root. A container six-inches wide by six-inches deep is the perfect size. Always correct in a ceramic pot and showy

The Basil Container

in a china cachepot, the container must be well-drained.

Prepare the seeds before you plant: Soak to soften for twenty-four hours in a glass bowl filled with warm water. Plant in rich potting soil, mixed three

How to Plant

parts earth to one part sharp sand for quick drainage. Place a layer of small stones in the bottom of the pot for drainage. Fill the container with soil almost to the top. Place twelve seeds on the surface spaced evenly apart. Sprinkle a quarter inch of soil over the seeds and tamp down lightly. Water thoroughly. Cover the container with plastic to create a terrarium environment. In two to three weeks, sprouts appear. Remove the covering. When the seedlings reach two-inches tall, select the hardiest three to nurture to maturity.

Place the terrarium in a warm, sunless spot until sprouts appear. Uncover. Move to bright, indirect light. At two-inches tall, move the

Light

three plants to their permanent home in a southern or western window to catch bright, direct sunlight.

Sweet basil likes to feel cozy. A temperature range of sixty-five to seventy-five degrees is ideal. If your plants feel too cold, they stop growing.

Temperature

The only condition your sweet basil plants find more disagreeable than the cold, is dry soil. Water the sprouts every four to five days. Water the mature

Water and Food

basil plants every three to four days to keep their soil evenly moist. To guarantee a bounty of green leaves, feed your friends quarter-strength liquid plant food with every other watering.

Five weeks in bright, direct sun finds your plants four-inches tall and ready to be enjoyed. (Harvesting promotes new growth.) Start the harvest by picking the leaves at the

When to Harvest

base of the third nodes. Pinch off flower buds to encourage bushy leaf growth and to delay bolting. A healthy sweet basil harvest lasts for at least twelve weeks.

The marriage of fragrance and flavor is the key to sweet basil's character. Sweet Basil Thai-Style Relish adds a splash of vibrant savor to grilled shrimp or blackened fish. Remember to have a crusty loaf on hand to sop the succulent sauce at meal's end.

Rinse the sweet basil under cold water. Pat dry. Coarsely chop.

Slice the cucumber in half, lengthwise. Remove the seeds and coarsely chop. Place in a medium bowl and sprinkle with salt. Set aside to dehydrate for thirty minutes.

Seed and dice the jalapeño pepper.

Coarsely chop the peanuts.

In a small bowl, combine the sesame oil and honey. Whisk to blend thoroughly.

Drain the cucumber. Discard the liquid.

Add all of the ingredients to the bowl of cucumber, except the sesame-honey mixture. Toss. Drizzle the honeyed sesame oil over all. Toss to coat.

Cover and chill in the refrigerator for thirty minutes before serving.

Stored in an airtight container in the refrigerator, the relish stays fresh for three to four days.

MAKES 4 SERVINGS [1 1/2 CUPS]

16 fresh sweet basil leaves

1 medium cucumber, peeled

1 teaspoon salt

1 fresh jalapeño pepper

2 tablespoons unsalted peanuts

2 tablespoons sesame oil

2 tablespoons honey

3 tablespoons minced red onion

2 tablespoons fresh lime juice

1 tablespoon rice vinegar

Instead of reaching for iodine or peroxide to topically medicate a minor injury, prepare an aromatic, antiseptic paste of sweet basil leaves and apricot kernel oil. Place the herb poultice on scrapes, painful hard-to-heal blisters, minor burns, and paper cuts to disinfect, reduce inflammation, and speed the healing process. This natural BandAid helps your body heal itself.

Rinse the sweet basil leaves under cold water. Pat dry. Mince the leaves.

In a small glass bowl, combine the basil and the apricot kernel oil. Mash to form a smooth paste.

Cut two rectangular strips of gauze large enough to cover the injury, plus an extra inch all around.

Spread an even layer of the basil paste on the surface of one of the gauze strips, leaving an inch around the edges free of paste to accommodate the surgical tape.

Place the clean strip of gauze on top.

Fasten the poultice to the injured area with surgical tape. Keep the healing balm on the injury for at least two hours.

Remove the poultice and discard.

Rebandage with plain gauze to keep the injured area clean and protected for the next twenty-four hours.

MAKES 1 TREATMENT [1/4 OUNCE]

8 fresh sweet basil leaves

1/8 teaspoon apricot kernel oil

Sterile cotton gauze

Surgical tape

Curly Chervil

Curly chervil is the pantry-potager's *herbe du jour* and an indispensable friend to all French chefs. Tossed with tarragon and parsley, it completes the essential French seasoning, *fines herbes.* Lacy leaves reveal curly chervil's close relationship to parsley. But curly chervil's flavor is sweeter and more refined. The fresh herb adds a hint of licorice to France's favorite chilled soup, vichyssoise. Don't be fooled by chervil's fragile appearance. Its curly fronds are as nutrient-rich, cleansing, and tonic as its big sister's, parsley (and as eager to flourish indoors). Curly chervil is a delicate dynamo. Bathe your tired, over-worked eyes in a mild infusion of just-picked leaves to revitalize and restore brightness.

Like its *Umbelliferae* sisters, parsley and dill, lacy-leaved

Botany, briefly

curly chervil (*Anthriscus cerefolium*) grows happily indoors all year. For successful germination, plant the little green seeds right away. They lose viability quickly. I recommend the variety, *Brussels Winter*.

Your curly chervil plants produce a large root system. A

The Chervil Container

terra-cotta container six-inches wide by six-inches deep gives them plenty of room to stretch out. Curly chervils don't need a fancy pot to shine, but they won't cooperate if the container lacks good drainage.

Prepare the seeds before you plant: Soak to soften for

How to Plant

twenty-four hours in a glass bowl filled with warm water. Plant in rich potting soil, mixed three parts earth to one part sharp sand for quick drainage. Place a layer of small stones in the bottom of the pot. Fill the container with soil almost to the top. Scatter two dozen seeds on the surface. Sprinkle a quarter inch of soil over the seeds and tamp down gently. Water throughly. Cover the container with plastic to create a terrarium environment. In two to three weeks, sprouts appear. Remove the covering. When the seedlings reach two-inches tall, select the nine hardiest to grow to maturity.

Place the seedling terrarium in a warm, sunless spot until sprouts appear. Uncover and move the nine plants to their permanent home in

Light

a northern window to catch indirect light all day.

Curly chervils favor a room temperature of sixty to seventy degrees. Keep your perky plants away from drafty windows. The

Temperature

fragile leaves suffer when exposed to the cold.

Your curly chervil plants like their soil kept evenly moist. Water the plants every three days. A cool, drink of quarter-strength liquid plant food twice-a-month

Water and Food

help your plants to produce a generous harvest.

Three to five weeks after sprouting, or when the plants reach four-inches tall, your curly chervils are ready to harvest. Pinch off the leaves with a gentle

When to Harvest

sideways tug at the base of the stalk. Harvest only the outer leaves, never pick from the growing center with the exception of the flowers. Nip them in the bud, as soon as they appear, to extend the harvest of pretty leaves for eight to ten weeks.

Curly Chervil Vichyssoise

Vichyssoise, once a summertime staple, is no longer savvy fare. (The classic potage *is practically all cream.) Instead of adding vichyssoise to a growing list of forbidden favorites, here's a wonderful, yogurt-based soup that's long on flavor but low on fat. Curly chervil seasons the velvety chilled soup with a whisper-sweet lick of licorice.*

Rinse the curly chervil under cold water. Pat dry. Mince and set aside. Slice the potatoes into half-inch cubes. Trim the leek, leaving an inch of firm, green top. Rinse thoroughly under cold water. Slice the leek into one-inch rounds.

In a heavy-bottomed pot, warm the olive oil over medium heat. Add the potatoes and leek. Sauté until the leek is translucent, about five minutes. Add three cups of water. Cover and bring to a boil. Lower the heat and simmer, partially covered, until the potatoes are tender, about twenty minutes. Whisk in the yogurt, half the minced chervil, salt, and pepper. Pour the mixture into a blender. Purée until smooth. Transfer to a covered soup tureen. Chill for two hours. Just before serving, garnish each portion with the remaining curly chervil.

MAKES 4 SERVINGS [4 1/2 CUPS]

14 fresh curly chervil sprigs

2 medium russet potatoes

1 large leek

1 tablespoon olive oil

1/2 cup plain nonfat yogurt

Salt and freshly ground black pepper to taste

Curly Chervil Eye Bath

Fluorescent lighting, air conditioning, ambient smoke, and hours spent squinting into the shining face of a computer screen strain your eyes to the limit. At the end of a long day, bathe your overworked peepers with a soothing chervil solution to reduce puffiness, restore clear vision and natural brightness.

Rinse the curly chervil under cold water. Pat dry. Place in a small glass bowl. In a small, nonmetal pot with a tightly fitting lid, bring the distilled water to a boil. Pour the boiling water over the chervil. Cover and steep for ten minutes. Place the cheese cloth in a fine-gauge mesh sieve. Strain the infusion into a clean glass bowl. Discard the spent herb. Set aside to cool to lukewarm. Fill the eye cup with the soothing solution. Tilt back your head to bathe your eye. Refill the eye cup and bathe the other eye. Repeat this procedure three times for each eye. Discard the unused eyebath. To get the most from this refreshing treatment, take time to rest with your eyes closed before resuming normal activity. (Eyecups are available from your local pharmacist.)

MAKES 1 TREATMENT [8 OUNCES]

10 fresh curly chervil sprigs

8 ounces distilled water

5-inch square cheese cloth

Eye cup

Garlic Chives

Cheery chives are a pleasure to cultivate. The garlic, or Chinese, variety are my choice for their champion performance indoors. The seeds seem sleepy at first but once these mini-onions take root, they grow like topsy. The savory flavor, reminiscent of garlic, is best-served as an Aromatic Sauce — a simple-to-prepare, simply delicious Asian-style raw sauce. (The tiny blossoms

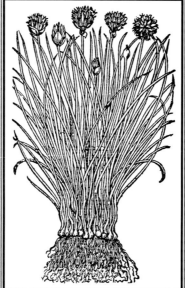

are tasty, too.) Garlic chives' earthy scent announces the presence of sulfur in the blade-like, dark-green leaves. A potent antioxidant and bacteria fighter, sulfur is the active healing agent in the Garlic Chive DecongeSteam treatment. Crew-cut harvest your garlic chives, trimming the leaves to within an inch of the soil, for six months of piquant abundance.

how to grow Garlic Chives indoors

Botany, briefly

Not unlike the variety of chives that you buy in the market, garlic, or Chinese chives (*Allium tuberosum*) are more interestingly flavored and easier to grow indoors. Store the small black seeds in a cool, dry place to stay fresh for months. Order the seeds by their common names, *Chinese* or *garlic chives*.

The Chives Container

Your Garlic chives grow "lawn-style" and do best in a long container with room to spread. Garlic chives like to grow tightly packed together. A rectangular terra-cotta container, seven-inches across and five-inches deep is just right. Of course, drainage is a must.

How to Plant

Prepare the seeds before you plant: Soak to soften for twenty-four hours in a glass bowl filled with warm water. Plant in rich potting soil, mixed three parts earth to one part sharp sand for quick drainage. Place a layer of small stones in the bottom of the container. Fill the pot with soil almost to the top. Scatter two dozen seeds on the surface. Sprinkle a quarter inch of soil over the seeds and tamp down lightly. Water thoroughly. Cover the container with plastic to create a terrarium environment. In about six weeks, sprouts appear. Remove the covering. When the seedlings reach two-inches tall, select the nine hardiest plants to nurture to maturity.

Light

Place the seedling terrarium in a warm, sunless place until sprouts appear. Uncover and move the nine plants to their permanent home in an eastern or southern exposure. They thrive in both bright, indirect or bright, direct light.

Temperature

Garlic chives are forgiving. The agreeable plants enjoy a wide temperature range from fifty-five to seventy-five degrees. But don't rely too much on your plants' insensitivity — keep them away from cold, drafty windows.

Water and Food

Garlic chives want their soil to dry out between waterings. Water every five to seven days. A light feeding of quarter-strength liquid plant food with each watering promotes a thick blanket of bright green leaves.

When to Harvest

Five to six weeks after sprouting, or when the plants reach four-inches tall, your garlic chives are ready to be enjoyed. Garlic chives grow in unison. Crew-cut-harvest, trimming the leaves to within an inch of the soil. After you harvest in this way, it takes a while for your chives to grow back. Move the plants to a cool spot in low light for a few days to stir new growth. Then return them to their permanent home for another piquant harvest.

Garlic Chive Aromatic Sauce

Dress salads, sauce vegetables, spread on crusty bread, swirl into soup — Garlic Chive Aromatic Sauce snaps with savory flavor. The sauce couldn't be easier to make. The classic combination of Asian seasonings practically blend themselves. The longer the sauce macerates, the brighter the taste. Just-picked and uncooked, garlic chives are at their tangy best.

Rinse the garlic chives under cold water. Pat dry. Mince and set aside.
Peel the daikon. Finely grate into a medium bowl.
Grate the lime peel. Add the lime zest to the daikon.
Squeeze the lime. Discard the seeds. Add the juice to the daikon-lime zest mixture.
Whisk in the sesame oil, rice vinegar, and soy sauce. Season with salt and pepper to taste.
Cover and set aside for thirty minutes to allow the flavors to develop.
Add the minced garlic chives. Stir to combine.
Serve at room temperature in little Asian teacups beside each dinner plate. Sauce to taste.

MAKES 2 SERVINGS [1/2 CUP]

12 fresh garlic chives

1 small daikon (Asian radish)

1 fresh lime

2 tablespoons sesame oil

2 teaspoons rice vinegar

2 tablespoons soy sauce

Salt and freshly ground black pepper to taste

Deep draughts of Garlic Chive DecongeSteam deliver healing vapor to infected nasal membranes. The minerals, sulfur and potassium, in garlic chive leaves, combined with gingerol, the active ingredient in ginger root, clear congested breathing passages, shrink swollen sinuses, and prevent a cold from spreading to your chest.

Rinse the garlic chives under cold water. Pat dry. Coarsely chop. Place in a large glass bowl. Peel the ginger. Add to the bowl of chives. In a large, nonmetal pot with a tightly fitting lid, bring the distilled water to a boil. Pour the boiling over the chives and ginger. Sit comfortably in a straight-backed chair with the Garlic Chive DecongeSteam in front of you. Drape a large terry towel over your head and shoulders to trap the steam. Lean over the rising vapor. Take slow deep breathes. If, at first, the hot steam is uncomfortable, lift the edge of the towel to adjust the temperature. Inhale slowly and deeply for ten minutes or until the water stops producing steam. Repeat the treatment twice a day, morning and evening, to clear your head and dry your sinuses.

MAKES 1 TREATMENT (32 OUNCES)

8 fresh garlic chives

1/2-inch slice fresh ginger root

32 ounces distilled water

Dill

To nurture your herb from window sill to place setting is to know the plant you're growing tastes good, looks good, and is good for you. Dill is essential living food. Its flowery-sweet flavor tastes and smells like springtime. A Scandinavian-style mingling of sharp and sweet, creamy and chunky, makes the Sunny Dill Dip delicious dipping for crisp, raw vegetables — and perfectly portable picnic fare. Gentle dill is a mild, but effective, digestive aid to quiet an upset stomach. Inhaling the celadon scent of freshly picked dill is as therapeutic as sipping the freshly steeped Dill Tummy Tea. Sunloving and fragrant, your dill plants' feathery jade fans ask for minimum care to perfume the air for many weeks.

Dill (*Anethum graveolens*) is aromatic, flavorful, and

Botany, briefly

extremely attractive. I recommend the compact, slow-to-bolt variety *Fernleaf.* The plant's medium-sized, light-brown seeds store well in a cool, dark place.

Feathery dill plants are right a home in a ceramic

The Dill Container

container. six-inches wide by six-inches deep. Dills' roots are delicate, far-reaching, and grow to fill the pot. Drainage is key to a healthy dill harvest.

Prepare the seeds before you plant: Soak to soften for

How to Plant

twenty-four hours in a glass bowl filled with warm water. Plant in rich potting soil, mixed three

parts earth to one part sharp sand for quick drainage. Place a layer of small stones in the bottom of the pot. Fill the container with soil almost to the top. Scatter a dozen seeds on the surface. Sprinkle an eighth inch of soil over the seeds and tamp down. Water thoroughly. Cover the container with plastic to create a terrarium environment. In about three weeks, sprouts appear. Remove the covering. When the seedlings reach two-inches tall, thin to the six hardiest plants to cluster in the center of the pot. Young dill plants are spindly and lean on each other for support as they mature.

Dill seeds need light to germinate. Place the terrarium in an eastern window to catch bright indirect light.

Light

Uncover. Move the six dill plants to their permanent home in a southern or western window to catch bright, direct sun.

Your dill plants live happily in a room temperature of sixty to seventy degrees. The tender, feathery leaves are disturbed by extreme cold.

Temperature

Keep the plants away from drafty windows.

Check the seedling terrarium every so often to maintain the moist enviroment. The mature plants, however, like to become dry between waterings. Water

Water and Food

them every five to seven days. A light feeding of quarter-strength liquid plant food with each watering keeps your plants perky and productive.

Four to five weeks after sprouting, or when the plants reach four-inches tall, the dills are an airy, blue-green bouquet. Snip the sprigs off at the stems with small

When to Harvest

kitchen shears. The dill harvest lasts about eight to ten weeks. When flowers appear let them go to seed. Harvest the seeds by gently shaking the flowers.

Sunny Dill Dip

*Sassy dill, spicy horseradish, and tangy lemon juice season the Norwegian-style dip to a tee. The creamy (happily lowfat) dressing complements the raw crunch of fresh **crudités**. Present classically on a serving platter with the dip taking center stage, or pipe the dip through a pastry bag with a star-shaped tip to decorate peppery radishes, fragrant fennel, and tender-sweet baby carrots.*

Rinse the dill under cold water. Pat dry. In a blender, combine the dill, yogurt, cottage cheese, and horseradish. Pulse until smooth, about thirty seconds. Transfer to a bowl. Add the lemon juice, cayenne pepper, salt, and black pepper. Stir to combine. Cover and set aside for thirty minutes to allow the flavors to develop. Serve at room temperature or lightly chilled. Stored in an airtight container in the refrigerator, the dip stays fresh for three to four days.

MAKES 4 SERVINGS [1 1/4 CUPS]

12 fresh dill sprigs

1/2 cup nonfat yogurt

1/2 cup lowfat cottage cheese

1 tablespoon creamed horseradish

2 teaspoons fresh lemon juice

1/8 teaspoon ground cayenne pepper

Salt and freshly ground black pepper to taste

Dill Tummy Tea

As a child, when my stomach ached from too much food, or too many treats, my Norwegian grandmother made me feel all better with a dose of freshly brewed dill tea. She called it "sunshine in a teacup." A cup of Dill Tummy Tea brings natural relief to a gaseous stomach without dampening your appetite. The tea, sipped slowly, is a cure for the hiccups, too. Dill Tummy Tea is good-food medicine.

MAKES 1 TREATMENT [8 OUNCES]

10 fresh dill sprigs
1-inch piece cinnamon stick
8 ounces distilled water
5-inch square cheese cloth

Rinse the dill under cold water. In a nonmetal teapot, combine the dill and the cinnamon stick . In a small nonmetal kettle, or covered pot, bring the distilled water to a boil. Pour the boiling water into the teapot. Set aside to steep for fifteen minutes. Place the cheese cloth in a fine-gauge sieve. Strain the Dill Tummy Tea into a ceramic mug. The delicate smell and charming flavor of Dill Tummy Tea is deceptive. This remedial tea is a digestive aid to be sipped slowly, not gulped quickly as one is tempted to do with a fine-tasting beverage. Retire to a comfortable place, sitting or reclining, to sip the quieting tonic. Take at least a half an hour to finish the mug of tea.

French Lavender

Not just a pretty fragrance, French lavender has healing flower power. The complex essential oil, extracted from the slender leaves and the cone-shaped spear of flowers, is renowned for its therapeutic properties. Calm your mind and your body, sip a soporific French Lavender Sleep Cocktail right before retiring and you drift off to dreamland in a state of scented relaxation. French lavender tastes as good as it smells. A sophisticated cooking herb, team French lavender with a full-bodied French burgundy for a distinctive, flavor-packed marinade. Growing French lavender indoors requires patience (and a little luck) but, stick with it, grateful Mother Nature rewards you tenfold.

how to grow French Lavender indoors

Of the three dozen species of lavender, French or fringed,

Botany, briefly

(*Lavendula spica*) is the indoor grower's friend. The tiny, midnight-brown seeds stay fresh for months in a cool, dry place. I recommend *Grosso,* the variety of French lavender that grows in the fields of the perfume capital of the world, Grasse.

Give your French lavender plants *joie de vivre.* A glazed

The Lavender Container

cachepot from Provençe, six-inches wide by six-inches deep, with good drainage, is *de rigueur.*

Prepare the seeds before you plant: Soak to soften for

How to Plant

twenty-four hours in a glass bowl filled with warm water. Plant in rich potting soil, mixed three parts earth to one part sharp sand for quick drainage. Place a layer of small stones in the bottom of the pot. Fill the container with soil almost to the top. Scatter two dozen seeds on the surface. Sprinkle a quarter inch of soil over the seeds and tamp down lightly. Water thoroughly. Cover the container with plastic to create a terrarium environment. In three to four weeks, sprouts appear. Remove the covering. When the seedlings reach two-inches tall, select the six hardiest plants to grow to maturity.

Place your seedling terrarium in a warm, sunless place until sprouts appear. Uncover. Move your little

Light

plants to a southern or western window to catch bright, direct light. French lavender flourishes in a full day of direct sunlight.

Your French lavender plants reward you with lots of fragrant leaves and flowers in a stable temperature

Temperature

range of sixty-five to seventy-five degrees.

French lavender plants like their soil to become dry between waterings. Water every five to seven days. A light feeding of quarter-strength liquid plant food

Water and Food

with each watering encourages a bounty of lavender blossoms. For an abundance of leaves, instead, cut the feedings to twice a month.

Three to five weeks after sprouting, or when your French lavender plants reach a height of four-inches, it's time to begin the harvest of leaves. Eight weeks later,

When to Harvest

the flowers make a fragrant appearance. Wait until they open before you harvest them. When harvesting lavender, pluck a whole stem rather than just the leaves or flowers. If properly cared for, your French lavender plants provide generously for months.

French Lavender & French Wine Marinade

Infused with a sprig of spirited French lavender and a splash of fruity French burgundy, this aromatic marinade deepens the flavor of whatever it macerates. The longer you marinate, the richer the flavor becomes. Nothing could be finer than the delicious taste of duck breast (or another strong-flavored meat), seasoned and tenderized in pungent French Lavender & French Wine Marinade.

Rinse the lavender sprig under cold water. Pat dry. Coarsely chop. Mince the garlic. In a small bowl, whisk to combine the wine, vinegar, olive oil, and honey. Season with salt and pepper. Add the lavender and the garlic. Stir to combine. In a shallow glass dish or baking pan, place the strong-flavored meat of your choice. (I recommend duck breasts.) Add the marinade. Turn the duck breasts to coat completely. Cover and refrigerate for at least two hours. Turn the breasts once or twice as they marinate. Remove the breasts from the marinade to cook. Transfer the marinade to a small bowl to use as a basting sauce.

MAKES 2 SERVINGS [1/2 CUP]

1 fresh lavender sprig

1 large clove garlic, peeled

1/4 cup red burgundy wine

1 tablespoon red wine vinegar

2 tablespoons extra virgin olive oil

1 teaspoon honey

Salt and freshly ground black pepper to taste

French Lavender Sleep Cocktail

Break the nerve-racking cycle of insomnia in a most delightful way — on sleepless nights, the French Lavender Sleep Cocktail is herbal relief to the rescue. Taken internally as a soporific elixir, lavender quiets an over-active mind (the primary cause of restless insomnia) and balances bouncing moods to banish feelings of anxiety.

Rinse the lavender leaves under cold water. In the glass jar, combine the lavender and vodka. Set aside in a cool, dark place for two weeks to extract the healing essences from the lavender leaves. Agitate the jar once a day. Place the cheese cloth in a fine-gauge sieve. Strain the tincture into the amber glass bottle. Discard the spent herb. In a small drinking glass, combine a half ounce of tincture and an ounce and a half of distilled water. Stir. Drink just before you retire. Repeat the procedure every night until your normal sleep pattern returns. Stored in the refrigerator, the bottle of tincture stays fresh for months. (Not recommended for children.)

MAKES 8 TREATMENTS [4 OUNCES]

60 fresh French lavender leaves
4-ounce glass jar with screw-top
4 ounces vodka
5-inch square cheese cloth
4-ounce amber glass bottle
  with screw-top
1 1/2 ounces distilled water

Ginger

Ginger has it all and does it all. Flavorful, aromatic, and therapeutic, ginger is essential to a hardworking pantry pharmacy. Absolutely indispensable to the healing-plant practitioner, the root is home to the plant's potent healing properties. A ginger-infused liniment brings penetrating warmth to muscles in spasm, stiff or swollen joints, and throbbing headaches.

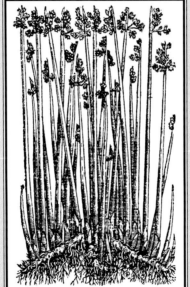

From a humble-looking piece of ginger root a miniature bamboo forest grows. While you wait for the ginger root to develop, your stand of aromatic ginger plants are busily producing delicately spiced leaves to chop into soups and salads. If you're a ginger groupie like me, I recommend trying the Ginger Julius Smoothie — a ginger-rich liquid luncheon.

how to grow Ginger indoors

Botany, briefly

Ginger (*Zingiber officinale*) is a perennial, propagated from its root-like rhizome. Available at any grocery store, choose a three-inch root that's satin-smooth, aromatic, and blemish-free. Like a potato, the ginger plant grows from little protruding nodes, called buds or eyes, on the root's surface.

The Ginger Container

Your ginger plants grow horizontally. A group of mature plants resemble a miniature bamboo forest. Choose a long clay container with room to spread. Seven-inches wide by five-inches deep is a perfect fit. Don't forget good drainage.

How to Plant

Prepare the ginger root before you plant: Place it in a paper bag in a warm, sunless spot. In about a week, several swollen growing-buds appear on the root's surface. Plant in a rich potting, soil mixed three parts earth to one part sharp sand. Place a layer of small stones in the bottom of the pot. Add two inches of soil. Set the root on the soil with the growing-buds facing up. Add more soil to cover the root and fill the container. Gently tamp down. Water very well. In about two weeks, bamboo-like spikes appear.

Light

Ginger responds beautifully to bright light but not hot sun. Place the potted ginger root in an eastern window to catch direct light in the morning, and bright, indirect for the rest of the day. This is your ginger plants' permanent home.

Temperature

Ginger grows wild in the damp tropical forests of Asia. To duplicate this steamy environment, place the plants in the warmest room in your house. Sixty-five to seventy-five degrees is ideal.

Water and Food

Ginger likes evenly moist soil with efficient drainage. Water every three days. Be sure the soil never dries out. Ginger plants benefit from a light feeding of quarter-strength liquid plant food with each watering.

When to Harvest

Two weeks after sprouts appear, or when your ginger plants reach four-inches tall, the harvest of fragrant leaves begins. (Each stem has six to eight leaves.) Pinch the leaves with a gentle sideways tug. After five months, the mature plants are a thriving mass of full-grown leaves. At this point, you can dig up the plants to harvest the spicy ginger roots. It's easy to start the ginger-growing cycle anew. Repeat these growing directions using a section of your newborn, homegrown rhizome.

Ginger Julius Smoothie

Fruit-frothy and ginger-cool, this rejuvenating and refreshing meal-in-a-glass restores flagging energy (and spirits). Ginger Julius Smoothie tastes terrific. Substantial enough to be a light lunch, it's my favorite midday pick-me-up.

Peel and grate the ginger root. Set aside. Rinse the strawberries under cold water. Remove the stems and leaves. Slice the banana.

In a blender, combine the strawberries, banana, orange juice, orange sorbet, yogurt, and grated ginger.

Purée until smooth, about one minute. Pour the Ginger Julius Smoothie into a chilled glass. Place a straw in the glass and serve.

MAKES 1 SERVING [1 1/2 CUPS]

1-inch slice fresh ginger root

4 strawberries

1/2 banana, peeled

1/4 cup fresh orange juice

1/3 cup orange sorbet

2 tablespoons nonfat yogurt

Ginger Liniment

Ginger Liniment is a healing massage oil. The remarkable ginger root, infused in oil, treats aching muscles, throbbing headaches, stiff joints, and back pain. Applied to the skin, the ginger liniment's penetrating action increases the flow of fresh blood, reduces swelling, and brings soothing warmth to the afflicted area.

Grate the ginger. Place it in the center of the cheese cloth. Gather the ends and twist to close. Wind the string around the top and tie a tight knot to make a ginger tea bag.

In a small, nonmetal saucepan with a tightly fitting lid, place the almond oil and the bag of ginger. Simmer over low heat for one hour. Remove from the heat and set aside to steep for one hour. Remove the bag from the oil. Before discarding, squeeze the bag gently into the saucepan to catch every precious drop of infused oil.

Use the funnel to transfer the liniment to the glass bottle. Pour some oil into your hands. Gently massage the afflicted area in a clockwise direction. Repeat the treatment twice a day until the symptoms disappear. Stored in a cool place, the bottle of liniment stays fresh for months.

MAKES 8 TREATMENTS (4 OUNCES)

2-inch slice fresh ginger root

5-inch square cheese cloth

1/2 yard of cotton string

4 ounces almond oil

Nonmetal perfume funnel

4-ounce amber glass bottle with screw-top

Italian Parsley

A bushy bunch of Italian parsley makes a dynamic, living centerpiece to fingertip harvest as you like it! Italian parsley's fresh, green-sweet flavor blends beautifully with garlic, olive oil, and pine nuts for a five-star Italian Parsley Pesto. The lacy green leaves are packed with phytochemicals and vital nutrients (iron, betacarotene, vitamin C, chlorophyll), all effective

fighters against anemia, gingivitis, swollen glands, and indigestion. A healing Italian Parsley Cleansing Tonic of juiced leaves balances and fortifies your system. Italian parsley, grown indoors, takes a bit longer to sprout than her sisters, cilantro and dill.

Be patient. In a little over a month, perky sprouts peek brightly out of the soil, the beginning of your three- month crop.

Italian, or flat leaf, parsley (*Petroselinum crispum*) is first

Botany, briefly

choice for pantry planting. Of the three common types, this one's flavor is strongest and sweetest. The tiny, midnight-brown seeds are gotten anytime of year and stay fresh for months when stored in a cool, dry place. For best results, I recommend the variety, *Gigante d'Italia*.

Your Italian parsley centerpiece lives happily in a

The Parsley Container

container that "breathes." Plant in a classic terra-cotta pot or ceramic cachepot with drainage. Select a container six-inches wide by six-inches deep.

Prepare the seeds before you plant: Soak to soften for

How to Plant

twenty-four hours in a glass bowl filled with warm water. Plant in rich potting soil, mixed three parts earth to one part sharp sand. Place a layer of small stones in the bottom of the pot. Fill the container with soil almost to the top. Scatter two dozen seeds on the surface. Sprinkle a quarter inch of soil over the seeds and gently tamp down. Water thoroughly. Cover the container with plastic to create a terrarium environment. In about four weeks, sprouts appear. Remove the covering. When the seedlings reach two-inches tall, select the nine hardiest to grow to maturity.

Place the seedling terrarium in a warm, sunless spot until sprouts appear. Uncover and move the nine hardy Italian parsley plants to

Light

their permanent home in a southern or western window to catch bright, direct sun.

Italian parsley plants thrive in a room temperature of sixty to seventy degrees. The delicate leaves are disturbed by extreme cold.

Temperature

Place the plants far away from drafty windows.

Italian parsley plants are always thirsty. Keep the soil evenly moist. Water every three days. A light feeding of quarter-strength liquid plant food with each

Water and Food

watering replenishes the hardworking plants.

Three to five weeks after sprouting, or when the plants reach four-inches tall with six mature leaves, your Italian parsleys are ready to enjoy. Pinch off the leaves

When to Harvest

with a gentle sideways tug at the base of the stalks. Harvest only the outer leaves, never pick from the growing centers, with the exception of the flowers. Pinch them back as soon as they appear to delay bolting. A contented crop performs beautifully for twelve weeks or more.

Traditionally paired with pasta, pesto is a tasty topping on simply-steamed new potatoes or dolloped as a finishing touch on hot or cold vegetable soup. For a change, enjoy the fresh flavor of Italian parsley, a sweet-and-savory variation on the classic, Italian-style basil pesto.

Rinse the Italian parsley under cold water. Pat dry. In a food processor, combine the parsley, garlic, and pine nuts. Process for thirty seconds. With the motor running, slowly add the olive oil. Blend until smooth.

Transfer to a bowl. Add the cheese, salt and pepper. Stir to combine thoroughly. Italian Parsley Pesto tastes its best served fresh at room temperature.

Stored in an airtight container, it keeps in the refrigerator for up to four days. You can also freeze individual portions to use as needed. Pour the pesto into an ice cube tray with eight sections, or into eight individual ice cube molds, about three tablespoons in each. Cover with plastic wrap. Italian Parsley Pesto stays fresh in the freezer for months.

MAKES 4 SERVINGS [1 1/2 CUPS]

20 fresh Italian parsley sprigs
2 large cloves garlic, peeled
1/2 cup pine nuts
1/2 cup extra virgin olive oil
1/2 cup freshly grated Romano cheese
Salt and freshly ground black pepper to taste

Italian Parsley Cleansing Tonic enhances your immune system, rejuvenates, and heals to keep your system balanced, clean, and clear. In other words, if you choose to drink only one health tonic, this is it! Italian parsley leaves are loaded with topnotch nutrients to boost energy, guard against low-grade infections, and aid digestion. One shouldn't drink more then two ounces of pure parsley juice. You're better off diluting it, as I do here, with carrot juice.

Rinse the Italian parsley under cold water. Pat dry. Discard any yellow leaves or damaged stems. Rinse the carrots under cold water. Cut off the leafy tops and discard. Slice the carrots into three-inch pieces. Process the Italian parsley, carrots, and lemon juice in the juicer. Serve at room temperature. Drink the cleansing tonic right away. Freshness and potency go hand-in-hand. Even though it tastes delicious, sip this strong beverage slowly. Anecdotal surveys report that pure herb juice sometimes causes upset tummies, so take at least a half an hour to drink it all.

MAKES 1 TREATMENT [8 OUNCES]

5 fresh Italian parsley sprigs

6 carrots

1 tablespoon fresh lemon juice

Lemon Balm

Crush a sprig of lemon balm between your fingers for a whiff of lemon heaven. The sparkling-clean scent is a complex mixture of mood-altering phytochemicals — lemon-scented citronella, rose-scented geranol, and lavender-scented linalool — prescribed by aromatherapists to uplift, inspire, and rejuvenate. Herbalists rely on the plant's antibacterial and antiseptic properties. Gargle with the Lemon Balm Honey Bee mouthwash to keep your mouth tingly-clean and your breath sweet. In the kitchen, lemon balm lends citrus snap to the honey-sweet taste and vinegar-sour flavor of Sweet & Sour Lemon Balm Sauce, the seasoning of choice for fresh-caught salmon (even tastier with a lemon balm sprig added to the poaching liquid).

how to grow Lemon Balm indoors

Botany, briefly

Lemon balm (*Melissa officinalis*) is the citrus-scented cousin of mint. Slow to germinate, once the bright-green, scalloped leaves sprout, the aromatic plants are off and running. The tiny dark-brown seeds are hardy. Keep them in a cool, dry place until you're ready to plant. Order the seeds by their common name, *Lemon balm*.

The Lem. Balm Container

Plant lemon balm in a simple, unglazed terra-cotta pot, six-inches wide by six-inches deep, to display the sweet, heart-shaped leaves. This bushy herb spreads to fill the growing space. Always plant your herbs in well-drained containers.

How to Plant

Prepare the seeds before you plant: Soak to soften for twenty-four hours in a glass bowl filled with warm water. Plant in rich potting soil, mixed three parts earth to one part sharp sand. Place a layer of small stones in the bottom of the pot. Fill the container almost to the top with soil. Scatter two dozen seeds on the surface. Sprinkle a quarter inch of soil over the seeds and gently tamp down. Water thoroughly. Cover the container with plastic to create a terrarium environment. In about six weeks, sprouts appear. Remove the covering. When the seedlings reach two-inches tall, select the hardiest six to grow to harvest.

Light

Place your terrarium in a warm, sunless spot until sprouts appear. Uncover and move the six lemon balm plants to their permanent home in a southern or western exposure to catch bright, direct sun.

Temperature

Lemon balm plants grow beautifully in a room temperature of sixty to seventy degrees. The fur-lined leaves are hardy, but are no protection for cold windows during winter months. Guard the plants against chill winds.

Water and Food

Your fragrant lemon balm plants like their soil to be evenly moist at all times. Water every three days. A light feeding of quarter-strength liquid plant food with each watering help the plants to grow.

When to Harvest

Six weeks after the first leaves appear, or when the plants grow to four-inches tall, the sweet-smelling harvest begins. Lemon balm plants get leggy. Your plants look best, and stay healthiest, when they're bushy. Pinch-harvest to keep them flourishing. If well tended, the fragrant harvest lasts for years.

Sweet & Sour Lemon Balm Sauce

Truly my own invention, with an aromatic lemon-balm soupçon for extra tang, Sweet & Sour Lemon Balm Sauce is based upon the familiar Provençal-style lemon topping. This delectable concoction is close to perfection, spooned over cold poached salmon. A delightful dipping sauce for steamed artichokes, too.

Rinse the lemon balm under cold water. Pat dry. Coarsely chop. In a small saucepan, over low heat, bring the sherry to a simmer. Add the honey and stir to dissolve. Whisk in the ginger, chicken broth, wine vinegar, and lemon zest. Season with salt and pepper. Simmer the lemony sauce for ten minutes, stirring. Serve Sweet & Sour Lemon Balm Sauce at room temperature.

MAKES 2 SERVINGS [1/2 CUP]

15 fresh lemon balm leaves

1/4 cup sherry wine

1 tablespoon honey

1/2 teaspoon minced fresh ginger root

1/4 cup chicken broth

2 tablespoons wine vinegar

1 tablespoon lemon zest

Salt and freshly ground black pepper to taste

Lemon Balm Honey Bee Mouthwash

Start the day with a burst of cooling flavor on your tongue and a clean, fresh feeling in your mouth. The lovely lemon scent of Lemon Balm Honey Bee Mouthwash lasts longer than the commercial kind (and tastes better, too). An effective bacteria fighter and antiseptic, lemon balm regulates the acid content of your saliva to help prevent tooth decay.

Rinse the lemon balm under cold water. Coarsely chop. In the glass jar, combine the lemon balm and the liqueur. Set aside in a cool, dark place for two weeks to extract the healing essences from the lemon balm leaves. Agitate the bottle once a day.

Place the cheese cloth in a fine-gauge sieve. Strain the tincture into a glass bowl. Discard the spent herb. Add the distilled water and honey. Whisk to dissolve the honey.

Transfer the Lemon Balm Honey Bee Mouthwash to the amber bottle.

Rinse or gargle twice a day with a half ounce of the cleansing mouthwash.

Stored in a cool place in the amber bottle, the mouthwash stays fresh for months.

MAKES 16 TREATMENTS [8 OUNCES]

25 fresh lemon balm leaves

2 ounces chartreuse liqueur

8-ounce glass jar with screw-top

5-inch square cheese cloth

6 ounces distilled water

1 teaspoon honey

8-ounce amber glass bottle with screw-top

Lemon Verbena

Lemon verbena is a botanical fuss pot and very difficult to grow from seed. Even in state-of-the-art greenhouses, the prima donna is cultivated from cuttings. Undaunted, I start with an organic seedling from my local nursery. Of all the aromatic citruses, the flavor, bouquet, and remedial value of lemon verbena are the strongest. The addition of its dynamic taste in the Lemon

Verbena Vinaigrette does wonderful things to a salad dressing standard. The sweet, clean floral scent is pure optimism (the state-of-mind in the Lemon Verbena PMS Massage). The leaves' high citral content is an antidote for the chronic complaints of premenstrual syndrome. Simply put, a lemon verbena plant is an essential member of my herb garden family!

how to grow Lemon Verbena indoors

Lemon Verbena (*Aloysia triphylla*) is terribly tricky to

Botany, briefly

grow from seed. There's no reason to struggle, or to exclude the super-citrus herb from your indoor garden. Simply, order three healthy young seedlings to nurture to harvest. Lemon verbena seedlings are available most of the year from nurseries and greenhouses. Order them by their common name, *Lemon verbena*.

As soon as you get them home, transfer your three little

The Verbena Container

plants to a ceramic pot, six-inches wide by six-inches deep. Your plants grow tall and aromatic in this roomy container with good drainage.

Plant in rich potting soil, mixed three parts earth to one

How to Plant

part sharp sand for good drainage. Place a layer of small stones in the bottom of the container. Add three inches of soil. Set the three seedlings on top. Fill in around them with tightly packed soil. Water to saturate the soil down to the roots. The newly transplanted, young seedling likes evenly moist soil right from the start.

To help them to adjust to their new home, place your freshly potted seedlings in an eastern exposure to get bright, indirect light.

Light

Remember, they're coming from a greenhouse environment where the climate is near-perfect. In a day or two, move the perky plants to their permanent home in a southern or western window to catch bright, direct sunlight.

Lemon Verbena thrives in a room temperature of sixty to seventy degrees. The hearty-looking, but delicate, leaves are disturbed by cold air.

Temperature

Keep the plants away from drafty windows.

Your lemon verbena want evenly moist soil at all times. The leaves get droopy when the plants are thirsty. Water every three days. A light feeding of quarter-

Water and Food

strength liquid plant food with each watering keeps the leaves green and fragrant.

Three to five weeks after you've transplanted your lemon verbena seedlings, or when the plants reach four-inches tall, the lemon-scented harvest begins. To keep the

When to Harvest

plants bushy and flourishing, pinch off the new-growth leaves at the base of the stalks. Do so, religiously, at least once a week, to reap four months of aromatic reward.

Lemon Verbena Vinaigrette

Salad dressing is the tie that binds the greens. Lemon verbena's assertive tart taste is showcased in Lemon Verbena Vinaigrette. Dress lettuces such as spunky frisée and spicy watercress, a peppery mixture that holds its own beside the sharp tang of citrus-spiked vinaigrette.

Rinse the lemon verbena under cold water. Pat dry. Mince the leaves. Mince the garlic. Mince the shallot. Chop the chives. In a small bowl, combine all of the ingredients except the olive oil. Whisk to combine. Slowly add the olive oil, whisking, until the dressing blends smooth. Dress your salad with just enough Lemon Verbena Vinaigrette to coat the greens lightly. A heavy coating of oil dulls the flavor of your fresh ingredients. Stored in the refrigerator tightly covered, the Lemon Verbena Vinaigrette stays fresh for a week.

MAKES 4 SERVINGS [1 CUP]

8 fresh lemon verbena leaves

1 clove garlic, peeled

1 small shallot, peeled

3 fresh chives

1/2 teaspoon salt

1/4 teaspoon freshly ground black pepper

2 tablespoons raspberry vinegar

1/2 cup extra virgin olive oil

Try not to let PMS cramp your style. At the first signs of discomfort, it's Lemon Verbena to the rescue. A healing self-massage with aromatic lemon verbena oil reduces tension, soothes tender breasts, relieves feelings of abdominal tightness, and beats the moody blues.

In a small bowl, combine the lemon verbena oil and the almond oil. Whisk to blend. Use the funnel to transfer the massage oil to the glass bottle. Retire to a comfortable place. Lie on your back. Take deep calming breaths to center yourself. Pour some oil into your hands. Rub them together to warm the oil. Place your hands on your belly. Press down gently. Slide your hands down the length of your abdomen then up toward your heart. Repeat several times. Gently press your solar plexus. Massage in a clockwise direction. Repeat the procedure on your lower abdomen. Reapply oil to your hands as needed. Gently massage oil into the side of each breast. If the pressure causes any feelings of discomfort, stop. Remember, the purpose of this treatment is to relieve stress, not cause it. Cover yourself with a blanket. Close your eyes and rest for at least ten minutes.

MAKES 1 TREATMENT [1/2 OUNCE]

8 drops lemon verbena essential oil

1/2 ounce almond oil

Nonmetal perfume funnel

Glass dropper

1/2 ounce glass bottle

Sweet Marjoram

Sweet marjoram is a graceful plant with soft green leaf clusters on slender purple stems. Sometimes called knotted marjoram, the velvety knobs on the tips of the stems look like tiny four-sided knots (impossible to untie). Sweet marjoram's delicious perfume — soft, mellow, and warm with a light eucalyptus-grove bottom note — is wonderfully effective

in a Sweet Marjoram Aromatherapy Bath for soothing away anxiety, calming frayed nerves, and centering yourself. The flavor of sweet marjoram is more complex and refined than its cousin oregano. At its fresh best, sweet marjoram's bright, piney taste plays cunning counterpoint to lush, tropical fruit preserves in the Marjoram Papaya Marmalade.

Sweet, or knotted, marjoram, (*Origanum majorana*) is unusually aromatic for a common kitchen herb. Sometimes confused with its botanical twin oregano, sweet marjoram, as its implies, is sweeter. Order the plant by its common names, *sweet marjoram* or *knotted marjoram*. The tiny seeds keep nicely in a cool, dry place, before planting.

Botany, briefly

Indoors, sweet marjoram plants grow in a green cascade of tender leaves. Plant them in a brightly glazed hanging container, six-inches wide by six-inches deep, with a drainage tray to prevent indoor water damage.

The Marjoram Container

To prepare the seeds before you plant: Soak to soften for twenty-four hours in a glass bowl filled with warm water. Plant in rich potting soil, mixed three parts earth to one part sharp sand. Place a layer of small stones in the bottom of the pot. Fill the container almost to the top with soil. Scatter two dozen seeds on the surface. Sprinkle a quarter-inch of soil over the seeds and gently tamp down. Water thoroughly. Cover the container with plastic to create a terrarium environment. In two to three weeks, sprouts appear. Remove the covering. When the seedlings reach two-inches tall, select the nine hardiest seedlings to grow to maturity.

How to Plant

Place the seedling terrarium in a warm, sunless spot until sprouts appear. Uncover and move your sweet majoram plants to their permanent home in a southern or western window to catch bright, direct sunlight.

Light

Sweet marjoram plants grow buoyantly in a room temperature of sixty-five to seventy-five degrees, similar to its mint relative, sweet basil. If your sweet marjoram plants feel cold, they stop growing. No cold drafts, please.

Temperature

Your sweet marjorams like their soil to dry out between waterings. Water the plants every five to seven days. A light feeding of quarter-strength liquid plant food with each watering encourages an extended harvest.

Water and Food

Five to six weeks after sprouting, or when the plants reach four-inches tall, your sweet marjorams are ready to harvest. Pinch-harvest to keep the plants bushy and productive. Nip off the flower buds as they appear to keep the leaf yield high. If properly tended, sweet marjoram flourishes for a sixteen-week harvest.

When to Harvest

Sweet Marjoram Papaya Marmalade

Yummy in the morning on buttered toast, or naughty after dark buttered on a slice of pound cake, Sweet Marjoram Papaya Marmalade, puts up elegantly in decorated canning jars to give as tropical treats for friends and family at winter holiday gift time.

Rinse the marjoram under cold water. Pat dry. Finely chop. Slice the papayas in half, lengthwise. Cut the fruit into small cubes. In a medium saucepan with a tightly fitting lid, combine the papaya, lemon peel, and lemon juice. Bring the mixture to a boil, stirring, until the fruit is translucent, about fifteen minutes. Stir in the sugar and marjoram. Continue to boil, stirring occasionally, until the marmalade thickens, about thirty minutes. Ladle the marmalade into the canning jars. Screw the lids on tight. Turn the jars upside down and set aside for five minutes. Turn them right side up and set aside to cool to room temperature. Label and date the jars. Stored in the refrigerator, the jars of marmalade stay fresh for two months.

MAKES 6 SERVINGS [3 CUPS]

25 fresh sweet marjoram leaves

2 ripe medium papayas, peeled and seeded

1 1/2 teaspoons grated lemon peel

1/4 cup fresh lemon juice

1 1/4 cups sugar

6 four-ounce canning jars, sterilized

Sweet Marjoram Aromatherapy Bath

Your sense of smell is the gateway to your sense of self. The healing essences in an aromatherapy bath enter your system through your pores and through your nose. The blend of essences in the Sweet Marjoram Aromatherapy Bath work in unison — marjoram balances, lemon balm lifts, and lavender calms. This bath is not a sleep potion, although it is the ultimate in relaxation. Instead, the effect is centering and head-clearing.

In a large, heavy-bottomed pot with a tightly fitting lid, combine the fresh marjoram and one quart of water. Bring to a boil. Lower the heat and simmer for five minutes. Turn off the heat and steep for fifteen minutes. Strain through a fine-gauge sieve into a glass pitcher. Discard the spent herb. Draw a comfortably warm bath. Pour the marjoram tub tea into the bath. Swirl the water to disperse the infusion. When the tub is almost full, add the essential oils. Agitate the water to combine the oils evenly. Lower yourself into the bath. Relax and float. Stay in the water for at least fifteen minutes to get the full benefit from this healing herbal soak.

MAKES 1 TREATMENT [32 OUNCES]

50 fresh sweet marjoram leaves

10 drops marjoram oil

10 drops lemon balm oil

8 drops lavender oil

Glass dropper

Mizuna

Mizuna is a pepper-flavored plant from Asia. Like its occidental counterpart, mustard greens, mizuna is a member of the large plant family brassica. Handsome-looking, indoor-flourishing, tender-leaved, and palate-pleasing, mizuna sends up slender white stems with delicate foliage. A stand-alone when it comes to salads, the leaves are a savory substitute for mustard greens in hearty Mizuna & Lentil Soup. The foliage contains impressive amounts of vitamin C, vitamin A, calcium, magnesium, and iron, the elements your body needs to keep the immune system humming. The tiny seeds are on the healing case, too. At the first sign of a cold, soak your feet in a Mizuna Footbath to stop the symptoms in their tracks.

Mizuna (*Brassica juncea*) are Japanese mustard greens.

Botany, briefly

Like their western relatives, the mustard plant, they're a member of the huge plant family, *brassica*. Mizuna are smaller and adapt easily to indoor horticulture. The dark-brown seeds are teensy. Keep them fresh in a dry tightly-covered container. Order the seeds by their common name, *mizuna*.

Grow your mizuna plants in a container, six-inches wide

The Mizuna Container

by six-inches deep. It won't be hard to find a colorful planter with Asian-style decoration to acknowledge the plants' heritage. Only one requirement: Good drainage.

To prepare the seeds before you plant: Soak to soften for

How to Plant

twelve hours in a glass bowl filled with warm water. Plant in rich potting soil, mixed three parts earth to one part sharp sand. Place a layer of small stones in the bottom of the pot. Fill the container almost to the top with soil. Scatter two dozen seeds on the surface. Sprinkle a quarter-inch of soil over the seeds and gently tamp down. Water thoroughly. Cover the container with plastic to create a terrarium environment. In two to three weeks, sprouts appear. Remove the covering. When the seedlings reach two-inches tall, select the six hardiest plants to nurture to harvest.

Place the seedling terrarium in a warm, sunless spot until

Light

sprouts appear. Uncover and move your mizuna plants to their permanent home in a southern or western window to catch bright, direct sunlight.

Mizuna are temperature-tolerant and adapt to a wide range

Temperature

of climates. Play it safe, place the container in a room temperature of sixty to seventy degrees. All plants grow sleepy in the cold.

Mizuna prefer evenly moist soil. Water every three to four

Water and Food

days. A light feeding of quarter-strength liquid plant food with each watering encourages a bountiful harvest of hot-and-spicy leaves.

Four weeks after sprouting, or when the plants are four-

When to Harvest

inches tall, your mizuna plants' peppery leaves are ready to pick. The mizuna rule: the more leaves you harvest, the more there are to harvest. Your mizuna plants' crop last for many months. To extend the leaf harvest, pinch away the flower buds as they appear. To harvest seeds, allow several flowers to grow to maturity. Gently shake the flowers for a shower of tiny seeds.

Fresh mizuna's hot-mustard tang is a tasty teammate for earthy lentils. Preserve the Asian herb's distinctive flavor and vital nutrients — quick-cook to wilt — three minutes or less.

Rinse the mizuna under cold water. Pat dry. Coarsely chop.

In a large, heavy-bottomed pot with a tightly fitting lid, combine the lentils, bay leaf, and water. Bring to a boil. Lower the heat and simmer, partially covered, until the lentils are soft, about forty-five minutes.

Chop the onion and tomatoes. Mince the garlic.

In a medium skillet, warm the oil. Add the onion and garlic. Sauté until the onion is soft, about five minutes. Add the tomatoes. Cook for five minutes.

Add the sautéed vegetables to the lentils. Add the mizuna. Stir to combine. Simmer to wilt the leaves, two to three minutes. Sprinkle vinegar over all to brighten the flavors. Add salt and pepper to taste.

Ladle the Mizuna & Lentil Soup into deep bowls. Serve piping hot.

MAKES 4 SERVINGS [5 CUPS]

40 fresh mizuna leaves

1/2 cup dried green lentils

1 bay leaf

4 cups water

1 small red onion

2 medium tomatoes

2 cloves garlic, peeled

2 tablespoons extra virgin olive oil

1 tablespoon red wine vinegar

Salt and freshly ground black pepper to taste

Mizuna Footbath

The Mizuna Footbath is an unusual, but extremely effective, way to treat and beat the early symptoms of a cold or bronchial flu. The skin on your feet is particularly sensitive and readily absorbs mizuna's healing elements. Like a liquid mustard plaster, the Mizuna Footbath stimulates circulation and encourages a cleansing sweat to rid the body of toxins.

In a large, heavy-bottomed pot with a tightly fitting lid, combine the mizuna leaves, seeds, and three quarts of water. Bring to a boil. Lower the heat and simmer, covered, for five minutes. Turn off the heat and set aside to steep overnight for extra strength. Heat the infusion to a comfortably hot temperature. Place the cheese cloth in a fine-gauge sieve. Strain the infusion into a large pitcher. Discard the spent herb.

Sit in a comfortable straight-back chair with the plastic basin at your feet. Fill half-way with the steaming infusion. Insert your feet. Add more liquid to submerge your ankles. Drape a bath towel over the top to trap the heat. Soak until the water begins to cool, about fifteen minutes. Vigorously rub your feet dry to stimulate circulation. Don cozy cotton socks.

MAKES 1 TREATMENT [3 QUARTS]

50 fresh mizuna leaves

1/4 cup mizuna seeds

5-inch square cheese cloth

Large plastic basin

Nasturtium

Parlor gardeners, home-healers, and adventurous cooks are rediscovering the remedial and nutritional generosity of nasturtium. An indoor champion, the plant produces tart-tasting foliage, edible honey-sweet flowers (a stellar garnish), and caper-flavored seeds. A cousin to watercress, nasturtium shares cresses' piquancy. Tuck the parasol-shaped leaves and open-faced blossoms into rice wrappers for Nasturtium Spring Rolls, a festive finger food. Nasturtium's moist leaves and vibrant flowers contain vitamin C and sulfur, both highly valued elements for stimulating the growth of new hair. After just a few treatments with Nasturtium Hair Rinse, your hair texture is thicker and stronger.

how to grow Nasturtium indoors

Nasturtiums' (*Tropaeolum majus*) tangle of vibrant orange

Botany, briefly

flowers and succulent green foliage look like an indoor meadow. The wrinkled, albino seeds keep well, stored in a cool, dry place. I recommend the compact, orange-flowered variety, *Dwarf Jewel*.

Nasturtium, like sweet marjoram, make a splash, hanging

The Nasturtium Container

in a sunny window. A container, six-inches wide by six-inches deep lets the pretty mess of leaves and flowers spread and thrive. Most hanging planters have drainage catchers to avoid indoor water damage.

Prepare the seeds before you plant: Soak to soften for

How to Plant

twenty-four hours in a glass bowl filled with warm water. Plant in rich potting soil, mixed three parts earth to one part sharp sand. Place a layer of small stones in the bottom of the pot. Fill the container almost to the top with soil. Place nine seeds, evenly spaced, on the surface. Cover with a half-inch of soil and gently tamp down. Water well to soak through. Cover the container with plastic to create a terrarium environment. In two to three weeks, sprouts appear. Remove the plastic wrap. When the seedlings reach two-inches tall, select the three hardiest nasturtium plants to bring to harvest.

Place your seedling terrarium in a warm, sunless spot until sprouts appear. Uncover

Light

and move the plants to their permanent home in an southern or western window to catch bright, direct sunlight.

Nasturtium develops successfully in a room temperature of sixty to seventy degrees.

Temperature

The sunset-orange blossoms are sensitive to extreme temperature change. Keep away from drafty windows.

Your nasturtium plants like the soil evenly moist. Water every three days. A light

Water and Food

feeding of quarter-strength liquid plant food with each watering produces an abundance of leaves, but discourages flower production. For a balanced ratio of flowers to leaves, feed twice a month.

Three to five weeks after sprouting, or when the vines are four-inches long, succulent

When to Harvest

foliage abounds. Soon after, flowers appear. Nasturtiums produce leaves and flowers simultaneously. When the flower petals drop, a cluster of three, caper-like seeds appear. For the tenderest leaves and sweetest flowers, harvest both as soon as they appear. Allow several flowers mature to harvest the spicy seeds. Your nasturtium harvest lasts for four productive months.

Hidden in these "rice paper" wrapped hand rolls are spicy nasturtium leaves, cool cucumber, juicy mango, lively mint, chewy rice noodles, and sweet flowers. Outstanding party food, Nasturtium Spring Rolls earn hostess kudos.

Rinse the nasturtium leaves, flowers, and the lettuce under cold water. Pat dry.

Peel the mango. Slice the fruit into eight equal pieces. Julienne-slice the cucumber.

In a medium bowl, rehydrate the vermicelli in boiling water, about two minutes. Drain.

Arrange all the ingredients on a platter beside a large bowl of warm water.

Place a wrapper in the water to rehydrate, about fifteen seconds. Lay it flat on a damp kitchen towel. Cover half the wrapper with a lettuce leaf. Top with two tablespoons of noodles, several cucumber strips, a mango slice, a nasturtium leaf, a flower, and two mint leaves. Fold the wrapper in half to close. Fold both ends in toward the center. Roll the wrapper up from the bottom, lengthwise, to form a tube.

Set aside on a platter.

Repeat the process for the remaining spring rolls. Well covered, the spring rolls stay fresh for about two hours.

MAKES 4 SERVINGS [8 SPRING ROLLS]

8 fresh nasturtium leaves

8 fresh nasturtium flowers

8 medium red lettuce leaves

1 small ripe mango

1 small cucumber, peeled

2 ounces dried rice vermicelli

16 fresh peppermint leaves

8 twelve-inch dried rice paper wrappers

Nasturtium Hair Rinse

Keep your hair strong and supple, dandruff-free, ph-balanced, and squeaky-clean with a once-a-week Nasturtium Hair Rinse treatment. Healthy, taut follicles are where thick, healthy hair is born. This concentrated flower water deep-cleans right down to the roots to stimulate the growth of fresh, young-looking new hair.

Rinse the nasturtium leaves and flowers under cold water. Pat dry. In a small, heavy-bottomed pot with a tightly fitting lid, combine the nasturtium leaves, nasturtium flowers, ginger, and the distilled water. Bring to a boil. Lower the heat and simmer for five minutes. Turn off the heat and steep for fifteen minutes. Strain through a fine-gauge sieve into a glass pitcher. Discard the spent herbs. Add the lemon juice. Stir. Wash your hair with your favorite shampoo. Finish with the Nasturtium Hair Rinse. Pour it on, finger-spread it through your hair evenly, and massage it into your scalp. Squeeze your hair to remove excess rinse. Dry and style in the usual way. Repeat the treatment once a week for a noticeable improvement in the texture of your hair.

MAKES 1 TREATMENT [16 OUNCES]

15 fresh nasturtium leaves

5 fresh nasturtium flowers

1/2-inch slice fresh ginger root

16 ounces distilled water

1 tablespoon fresh lemon juice

Peppermint

Popular peppermint is renowned for its all-around healing properties — antiseptic, cleansing, anti-inflammatory, anesthetic, astringent, and stimulating. The mighty mint's powers come from essential menthol — a wonder-ingredient for

the care of all skin types. Nothing is easier to prepare, or to apply, than a Mint Mousse Facial mask (and the results are immediately visible and satisfying). This tingling skin food tones, tightens, and refines the delicate texture of your face. Everyone agrees — the flavor of peppermint is delectible. The refreshing refresco, Peppermint Kiwi Granita, serves appetizingly before dinner, formally between courses, and traditionally for dessert (or anytime).

how to grow Peppermint indoors

Peppermint (*Mentha piperita*) is the mintiest of the many

Botany, briefly

mints. The small, dark seeds are easy to come by and keep indefinitely stored in a cool, dry place. I recommend the variety, *Blue Balsam*, for the leaves' deep-peppermint flavor.

Pert peppermint plants grow happily in a container six-

The Peppermint Container

inches wide by six-inches deep. Feel free to be imaginative in your choice of container, as long as it's well-drained. Lovely peppermint sets off any style planter.

Prepare the seeds before you plant: Soak to soften for

How to Plant

twenty-four hours in a glass bowl filled with warm water. Plant in rich potting soil, mixed three parts earth to one part sharp sand. Place a layer of small stones in the bottom of the pot. Fill the container almost to the top with soil. Scatter two dozen seeds on the surface. Sprinkle a quarter-inch of soil over the seeds and gently tamp down. Water well to soak through. Cover the container with plastic to create a terrarium environment. In two to three weeks, sprouts appear. Remove the plastic wrap. When the seedlings reach two-inches tall, select the six hardiest peppermint plants to grow to maturity.

Place the seedling terrarium in a warm, sunless spot until sprouts appear. Uncover and move your peppermint plants to their permanent

Light

home in a southern or western window to catch bright, direct sunlight.

Peppermint is hardy, living well in a room with an average temperature range of sixty to seventy degrees. Keep the leaves away from

Temperature

direct contact with window glass. They dislike extreme heat or cold.

In the wild, peppermint grows beside brooks and streams. Indoors your plants want to maintain evenly moist soil. Water every three to four days. A light drink of

Water and Food

quarter-strength liquid plant food with each watering boosts leaf production noticeably.

Four to five weeks after sprouting, your peppermint plants are full and lush. Begin your harvest with the larger leaves. Peppermint gets leggy, so pinch off the leaf

When to Harvest

clusters, growing at the top to encourage bushiness. Although the little pink flowers are very charming, nip out the flower buds when they appear to extend your leaf harvest. Perennial peppermint produces a minty-fresh harvest for many months.

Glacial Peppermint Kiwi Granita — soft as a snow ball, smooth as cream, made with crisp, fresh peppermint leaves, sweet and tart-on-the-tongue kiwi, and lip-puckering lime — is a fabulous frozen concoction to temper your palate before, during, or after spicy feed.

Rinse the peppermint under cold water. Pat dry. Coarsely chop eight leaves. Slice the kiwis into half-inch rounds. Grate one lime. Set the zest aside. Juice both limes. Place the kiwis in the blender to purée, about one minute. Add the chopped peppermint, lime zest, lime juice, and sugar. Blend until smooth. Pour the fruit purée into a mesh sieve and strain into a flat, freezer-proof pan. Place in the freezer, until ice crystals form, about two hours. Scrape the surface of the granita with a fork to flake into fluffy snow. If the granita is not frozen to the bottom, return to the freezer for another hour. Fluff with a fork. Spoon into two chilled cocktail glasses. Garnish each with a mint leaf and serve. Stored in the freezer, covered with plastic wrap, the granita keeps for about four hours before serving.

MAKES 4 SERVINGS [2 CUPS]

12 fresh peppermint leaves

12 ripe kiwis, peeled

2 fresh limes

1/2 cup sugar

Peppermint Mousse Facial

A peppermint infusion whipped stiff with egg whites is a cosmetic mousse (good enough to eat) that clarifies, tones, and tightens the texture of your skin. This minty mask leaves your face soft and glowing.

MAKES 1 TREATMENT [1 OUNCE]

8 fresh peppermint leaves

1/2 ounce distilled water

1 raw egg

Rinse the peppermint under cold water. Pat dry. Finely mince the leaves. Place in a small glass bowl. In a small nonmetal pot with a tightly fitting lid, bring the distilled water to a boil. Pour the boiling water over the peppermint. Cover and steep for fifteen minutes. In a small glass bowl, separate the egg white. Save the yolk for another use. Beat to stiffen into peaks. Fold in the peppermint infusion, including the leaves. Beat for another fifteen seconds to re-stiffen. Apply the mask to clean, dry skin. Spread a generous, even layer to cover the face and neck. Avoid the sensitive skin around the eyes. Leave the mask on to dry and tighten, about fifteen minutes. To remove the mask, splash ice cold water on the skin until it feels completely clean. Finish with a thin layer of your favorite moisturizer. Repeat the treatment as often as you like — oily skin types benefit from frequent applications.

Rosemary

Rosemary remembers. The arousing aroma of rosemary triggers memories and enhances the ability to recall minute details and long-forgotten facts. Need to think up a good idea? Bruise the evergreen needles to release the resinous scent. The inspiring perfume excites a flurry of creative brain activity. In fact, rosemary is so stimulating, avoid its use in the evening — it may cause sleeplessness.

Aerate the area with a fragrant spray of Rosemary Room Mist when you're on the brink of a cold, feeling sluggish, or stressed-out. The flavor of rosemary is a favorite of mine. I feature the herb in Rosemary Savory Custard, a little side dish with a big taste. (Be sure to make enough to offer seconds.)

Rosemarys' (*Rosmarinus officinalis*) leaves are aromatic,

Botany, briefly

evergreen needles; the flowers are tiny, blue blossoms. The pointy, chocolate-brown seeds are small and don't germinate unless they're very fresh. Plant many and as soon as they arrive. Outdoors, rosemary is a three-feet shrub. Indoors, I recommend *Santa Barbara,* a small variety that grows to spread horizontally.

Rosemary matures into handsome savory-scented plants in

The Rosemary Container

a container six-inches wide by six inches deep. Grow the miniature, evergreen shrublets in a round bowl (with a drainage hole) to simulate a bonzai-style planting.

Prepare the seeds before you plant: Soak to soften for

How to Plant

twenty-four hours in a glass bowl filled with warm water. Plant in rich potting soil, mixed three parts earth to one part sharp sand. Place a layer of small stones in the bottom of the pot. Fill the container almost to the top with soil. Scatter five dozen seeds on the surface. Sprinkle a quarter-inch of soil over the seeds and gently tamp down. Water thoroughly. Cover the container with plastic to create a terrarium environment. In four weeks, sprouts appear. Remove the plastic wrap. When the seedlings reach two-inches tall, select the six hardiest rosemary plants to grow to maturity.

Place the seedling terrarium in a warm, sunless spot until sprouts appear. Uncover and move your rosemary plants to their permanent

Light

home in a southern or western window to catch bright, direct sunlight.

Rosemary grows lovely in a room temperature of sixty to seventy degrees. Keep the plants away from direct contact with window glass.

Temperature

Rosemary dislikes extreme heat or cold.

Rosemary plants live comfortably in evenly moist soil. Water every three to four days. Feed rosemary sparingly, a light drink of quarter-strength liquid

Water and Food

plant food, once a month, keep the plants hale and hearty.

Five to six weeks after sprouting, or when your rosemary plants are four-inches tall, the fragrant harvest starts. In the beginning, when the young plants resemble

When to Harvest

bottle brushes, pinch the growing tips to encourage bushiness. As the plants mature, they grow to become more like scruffy shrubs. At this stage, harvest by pinching off whole sprigs. Give your robust rosemary plants loving care and they reward you with a lifetime of savory goodness.

Rosemary Savory Custard

A side dish that won't play second fiddle, Rosemary Savory Custard is something out of the ordinary. The secret for a distinct but delicate rosemary flavor — a slow-simmered milk infusion of rosemary with a garlic kick.

Rinse the rosemary under cold water. Pat dry.
Preheat the oven to 300° F.
Coat four, four-ounce ramekins with butter. Set aside.
In a medium saucepan, combine two rosemary sprigs, garlic, and milk. Simmer over low heat until the milk reduces to one cup, about fifteen minutes.
Strain the aromatic, infused milk into a large bowl.
Discard the rosemary and garlic.
Add the egg and yolks, salt, pepper, and nutmeg.
Mix to blend thoroughly.
Fill each ramekin with the mixture.
Place the ramekins in a baking pan. Place the pan in the oven. Pour several inches of hot water into the pan to create a *bain marie*.
Bake the ramekins in the water bath until a toothpick inserted in the center of each custard comes out clean, about forty-five minutes.
Remove the pan from the oven.
To serve, turn out each custard on its own plate.
Garnish each with a sprig of rosemary.

MAKES 4 SERVINGS [2 CUPS]

6 fresh rosemary sprigs

1 tablespoon butter

2 cloves garlic, peeled

1 1/2 cups whole milk

1 raw egg

2 egg yolks

1/4 teaspoon salt

1/4 teaspoon white pepper

1/8 teaspoon nutmeg

Rosemary Room Mist

Clear the air with Rosemary Room Mist. The bracing vapor makes you feel well psychologically and physically. The forest-fresh scent is mood elevating and medicinal, uplifting and antiseptic. The herb's active ingredient is the volatile oil, camphor. The healing resin disinfects the air, relieves tension headaches and the sniffles, and is an antidote for stress and depression.

Rinse the rosemary under cold water. Pat dry.
In the glass jar, combine the rosemary and alcohol.
Set aside in a cool, dark place for two weeks to
extract the healing essences from the rosemary.
Agitate the jar once a day.
Place the cheese cloth in a fine-gauge sieve.
Strain the rosemary tincture into the spray bottle.
Discard the spent herb.
Add the distilled water.
Shake the bottle gently.
For healing: Spray the sickroom every two hours.
For inspiration and well-being: Spray as required.
Shake the bottle gently before each use.
Stored in a cool, dark place, the bottle of room mist
stays fresh for months.

MAKES 1 SPRAY BOTTLE [16 OUNCES]

15 fresh rosemary sprigs

8-ounce glass jar with screw-top

8 ounces isopropyl alcohol

5-inch square cheese cloth

16-ounce plastic spray bottle
with pump-handle screw-top

8-ounces distilled water

Sage

Sun-loving, abundant, aromatic, and undemanding, versatile sage is a low-maintenance addition to your pantry planting. The warm and wonderful taste of sage is perfect for flavoring the ultimate comfort food — Sage-Stuffed & Twice-Baked Potatoes. The fresh leaves are especially mellow-flavored, simply sauteed with onion, garlic, and a dollop of creamy yogurt.

Cozy the sage plant close to the other herbs. The fuzzy, grey-green leaves stand guard against airborne plant diseases and repel insects. Sage represents herbal healing at its most reliable (its botanical Latin name, Salvia, means "to heal"). Mist your throat, or gargle, with Sage Throat Spray to treat canker sores, thrush, tonsillitus, and irritated gums.

how to grow Sage indoors

Sage (*Salvia officinalis*) is another member of the mint

Botany, briefly

family. For a harvest of delicious, fragrant leaves, I recommend the variety, *Golden Sage*. This pretty plant doesn't flower, instead it focuses all of its energy on producing spicy leaves. The sable-brown seeds are easy to come by and store efficiently in a cool, dry place until you're ready to plant.

Sages' long, soft leaves look lovely in a white-glazed

The Sage Container

basket-weave container. Select a cachepot, six inches by six inches (the tried-and-true size.)

Remember your decorative pot must have a drainage hole.

Prepare the seeds before you plant: Soak to soften the hard

How to Plant

little seeds for thirty-six hours in a glass bowl filled with warm water. Plant in rich potting soil, mixed

three parts earth to one part sharp sand. Place a layer of small stones in the bottom of the pot. Fill the container almost to the top with soil. Scatter two dozen seeds on the surface. Sprinkle a quarter-inch of soil over the seeds and gently tamp down. Water well to soak through. Cover the container with plastic to create a terrarium environment. In two to three weeks, sprouts appear. Remove the plastic wrap. When the seedlings reach two-inches tall, select the six hardiest sage plants to bring to harvest.

Place the seedling terrarium in a warm, sunless spot until sprouts appear. Uncover

Light

and move your sage plants to their permanent home in

a southern or western window to catch bright, direct sunlight.

Sage plants are temperature-tolerant and adapt to a wide range of climates. For best

Temperature

performance, place the plants in a room with a

temperature range of sixty to seventy degrees.

Sage plants require the soil to dry out between waterings. Water every five to seven

Water and Food

days. Sage relish a light feeding of quarter-strength liquid plant food with

every watering to keep leaf production high.

Four to five weeks after sprouting, or when plants are four-inches tall, the young

When to Harvest

leaves are ready to harvest. If you follow my advice and plant a nonflowering

variety of sage, you won't be bothered by early bolting. However, sage plants do tend toward legginess. Pinch-harvesting is a must to encourage bushy growth. If carefully tended, your sage plants provide a hearty harvest for months.

Sage-Stuffed & Twice-Baked Potatoes

There's no law that states, "Thanksgiving stuffing must go inside a turkey." Better for you, and better tasting, too — scrumptious sage-stuffed spuds are in a class all their own and a meal by themselves.

Preheat the oven to 375° F. Rinse the sage and parsley under cold water. Pat dry. Finely chop. Prick the potatoes with a fork. Place on a baking sheet. Bake for an hour and a quarter. Mince the garlic. Chop the onion. In a skillet, heat the olive oil. Add the garlic and onion. Sauté to golden and soften, about three minutes. Add the sage and parsley. Sauté one minute to wilt. Remove from the heat and set aside. Slice open the baked potatoes, lengthwise. Remove the potato carefully to keep the jackets intact. In a medium bowl, mash the potato with a fork. Add the sage sauté and the yogurt. Season with salt and pepper. Mix thoroughly. Stuff the potato jackets with the sage filling. Place on the baking sheet. Return to the oven to bake until heated through and browned, about fifteen minutes. Serve piping hot.

MAKES 4 SERVINGS [ABOUT 4 CUPS]

8 fresh sage leaves

4 fresh Italian parsley sprigs

4 medium Idaho potatoes

2 cloves garlic, peeled

1 small onion, peeled

2 tablespoons extra virgin olive oil

1/4 cup nonfat yogurt

Salt and freshly ground black pepper to taste

Sage Throat Spray is strong herbal medicine. Sage is credited with healing everything from the night sweats to epilepsy. The inside of the mouth is especially receptive to the plant's antiseptic action. Administered as an infused spray, sage reduces painful swelling and brings welcome relief to a sore, inflamed throat.

Rinse the sage under cold water. Pat dry. Place in a small glass bowl. In a small, nonmetal pot with a tightly fitting lid, bring the distilled water to a boil. Pour the boiling water over the sage. Cover and steep for ten minutes. Place the cheese cloth in a fine-gauge sieve. Strain the infusion into the spray bottle. Discard the spent herb.

For swollen, inflamed throat: Apply the spray every two hours.

For irritated or tickly throat: Apply the spray three times a day — morning, afternoon, bedtime. Stored in the refrigerator, the bottle of throat spray stays fresh for several days. After three days, discard the unused infusion and make a fresh supply.

MAKES 1 SPRAY BOTTLE [8 OUNCES]

5 fresh sage leaves

8 ounces distilled water

5-inch square cheese cloth

8-ounce amber glass bottle
   with spray-top

Thyme

A cachepot of cascading thyme, at home in your kitchen window, is a culinary treasure. The taste of the fresh herb is a world-of-flavor away from the dried variety. The energetic savor of fresh thyme is stronger and more complex (with a particular ability to blend and brighten diverse flavors). Delicious sweet or sharp, thyme and tomatillos team with sass and spine

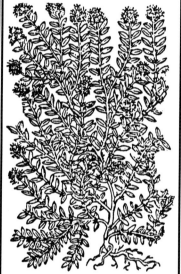

in Thyme Salsa Verde (you'll want to use it on top of everything). Like its herb sisters in the mint family, healing fresh thyme is anti-inflammatory, antiseptic, and rich in phytominerals. Turn to soothing Thyme Cough Drops (a sugary concentrate of infused thyme baked into lozenges) to turn off coughing, reduce swelling, and dry decongested lungs.

Thyme (*Thymus vulgaris*) has more than one hundred

Botany, briefly

varieties with dozens of flavorful scents from lemon frost to caraway. My choice is, *Narrowleaf French*, with its low-growing, cascade of gray-green leaves, and piquant flavor. The tiny, dark-brown seeds are easy to find, easy to store, and eager to germinate.

Thyme plants demand good drainage. Your plants grow

The Thyme Container

contentedly in a porous clay pot, six-inches wide by six-inches deep. Look for an unglazed terra-cotta cube for dramatic display.

Prepare the seeds before you plant: Soak to soften for

How to Plant

twenty-four hours in a glass bowl filled with warm water. Plant in rich potting soil, mixed three parts earth to one part sharp sand. Place a layer of small stones in the bottom of the pot. Fill the container almost to the top with soil. Scatter two dozen seeds on the surface. Sprinkle a quarter-inch of soil over the seeds and gently tamp down. Water well to soak through. Cover the container with plastic to create a terrarium environment. In three to four weeks, sprouts appear. Remove the plastic wrap. When the seedlings reach two-inches tall, select the six hardiest thyme plants to nurture to maturity.

Place the seedling terrarium in a warm, sunless spot until

Light

sprouts appear. Uncover and move your thyme plants to their permanent home in a southern or western window to catch bright, direct sunlight.

Thyme thrives in a room temperature range of sixty to

Temperature

seventy degrees. To keep your plants warm on chilly winter nights, leave a night light burning nearby.

Your thyme plants like the soil to dry out between

Water and Food

waterings. Water every five to seven days. Your thyme plants appreciate a light feeding of quarter-strength liquid plant food with every watering to enchance growth and fragrance.

With thyme it's simple. Four to six weeks after sprouting,

When to Harvest

or when the plants are four-inches tall, it's thyme to harvest. As your thyme plants grow to maturity, they become leggy. To keep your plants bushy and beautiful, harvest whole sprigs. Don't pick individual leaves. Enjoy harvesting this healing perennial for up to two years.

Thyme Salsa Verde

The green-pepper bite of thyme puts extra zip in Mexican-style, mild-alarm salsa verde (green sauce). Best-presented in a glazed terra-cotta bowl for diners to enjoy al gusto — sauce enchiladas on their way to the oven, drizzle a spicy ribbon on sweet corn chowder, or serve on the side with sizzling crab cakes.

Rinse the thyme under cold water. Pat dry. Remove the leaves from the stems. Discard the stems. Coarsely chop. Set aside. Coursely chop the onion. In a large, heavy-bottomed pot with a tightly fitting lid, combine the tomatillos, chilies, one teaspoon of salt, and four cups of water. Bring to a boil. Lower the heat and simmer, uncovered, until the tomatillos are tender, about ten minutes. Drain. Transfer to a blender. Add the thyme, onion, and garlic. Purée until smooth. In a large skillet, warm the oil. Add the purée. Cook, stirring, until thick and dark, about five minutes. Add the broth. Return to a boil. Reduce the heat and simmer until the salsa coats a spoon, about ten minutes. Season with the remaining salt. Stored in the refrigerator tightly covered, the salsa stays fresh up to four days.

MAKES 4 SERVINGS [2 CUPS]

3 fresh thyme sprigs

10 fresh tomatillos, husked

1 small onion, peeled

2 jalapeño chilies

2 1/2 teaspoons salt

2 cloves garlic, peeled

1 tablespoon vegetable oil

1 cup chicken broth

Thyme-infused lozenges made kitchen-fresh — the herb-green, healing pastilles are gentle relief to calm a nagging cough.

Rinse the thyme under cold water. In a small, heavy-bottomed pot with a tightly fitting lid, bring the thyme and the distilled water to a boil. Lower the heat and simmer for five minutes. Set aside to steep overnight. Coat an eight-inch-square cake pan with two teaspoons of butter. Set aside. Coat a medium, heavy-bottomed pot with the remaining butter. Strain the thyme infusion into the pot. Discard the spent herb. Add the sugar, corn syrup, oil of orange, and cream of tartar. Stir to dissolve the sugar. Cook over medium-high heat, moving the pot in a circular motion to swirl the liquid until it boils. Take the temperature. Swirl-cook at a boil, until the thermometer reads 300° F. Pour the syrup into the cake pan. Set aside about five minutes. Score the semi-hard syrup into half-inch squares with a knife. Set aside to harden, about thirty minutes. Turn out on a sheet of waxed paper. Break into cough drops along the scored lines. Stored in an airtight container, the Thyme Cough Drops stay fresh for months.

MAKES 240 COUGH DROPS [18 OUNCES]

4 fresh thyme sprigs

16 ounces distilled water

1 tablespoon unsalted butter

1 cup sugar

1/4 cup light corn syrup

1 teaspoon oil of orange

1 teaspoon cream of tartar

Candy thermometer

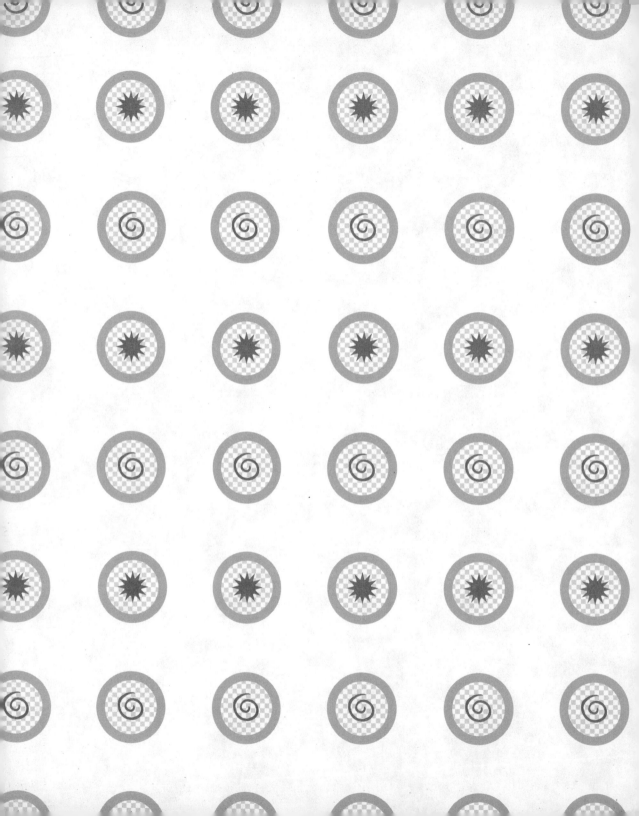